AF496795

Working with your family

NOÉMIE KEIME

NOÉMIE KEIME

Working with your family

3-step reflection on whether the family business is right for you

ISBN: 978-2-9584089-0-9

EAN: 9782958408909

Download the audiobook

for free!

Read this first.

Just to thank you for buying my book,

I would like to offer you the 100% FREE audiobook version!

To download it, go to:

https://bit.ly/3yF6w6N

Introduction

If you bought this book, it's probably because you feel alone in your thinking. A multitude of unanswered questions must be jostling in your mind. "Am I made to take over the family business?", "Is this really what I want to do?", "what will happen if it goes wrong?" are just a few examples of the questions that probably inhabit you. You are probably trying to talk with those around you about this dilemma that is pulling you, but no one really seems to understand the importance of this project and its complexity. So you keep reflecting on all these questions by telling yourself that you're alone in this situation. But you're never alone.

In Canada, 63.1% of private businesses are family-owned, or two-thirds of Canadian private sector companies. They represent half of the gross domestic product of this sector[1]. For 63.1% of Quebec family businesses, family succession is one of the most important objectives. Yet very few are planning[2] this event. In France, 83% of companies in 2016 were family-owned. Of this percentage, 58% plan to pass on management or leadership

---

[1] BASSETT ET FORBES, *The Economic Impact of Family-Owned Enterprise in Canada*, 2019, [Online], URL address : https://familyenterprise.ca/wp-content/uploads/2020/01/CBOC-2019-Family-Owned-Enterprises-Impact-Report.pdf

[2] CISNEROS, L., HAMON, G., VEILLEUX, A., GUILIANI, F., IBANESCU, M., *L'album de familles — enquête statistique sur les entreprises familiales québécoises 2020*, Familles en affaires — HEC Montréal, 2021

to the next generation. But only 14% have a robust, formal and communicated[3] succession plan.

These statistics can be found across the Atlantic and around the world. You're certainly not the only person asking yourself all these questions; you just haven't found the community with the same echo.

During my last university year, I had the chance to participate in the first edition of the Circuit – On the Way to the Next Generation[4] program offered by Familles en affaires HEC Montréal[5]. The Circuit aims to help students who come from business families to equip themselves to know if they want to work in their family businesses, what this entails, and if their ultimate goal would be to take over the family business or to launch an entrepreneurial project within it. Each session lasted about 3 hours and consisted of two parts. The first of the sessions was often theoretical, taught by a professor or a specialist in the subject. We were talking about one or more technical and singular concepts of families in business. During the second part, someone would come to testify about their experience with the subject of the session and answer our questions. For 6 months, we had the chance to work on 6 different themes and enjoy a dozen testimonials. In addition, the Circuit has created a community of people who experience the same thing at similar or different stages in their journey to take over the family business. We were able to share our doubts, challenges and experiences, which allowed us to move forward in our personal reflections. This program was an incredible opportunity that allowed me to consciously choose to join my family in our company. Knowing the challenges I would face and the opportunities that my commitment would

---

[3] KINDERMANS, M., *BPI France se mobilise pour la survie des entreprises familiales*, Les Échos, 2020, [Online], URL address: https://www.lesechos.fr/pme-regions/actualite-pme/bpifrance-se-mobilise-pour-la-survie-des-entreprises-familiales-1162454

[4] Familles en Affaires, *Circuit – Sur la voie de relève*, Famille en Affaires, HEC Montréal, 2021, [Online], URL address :
https://famillesenaffaires.hec.ca/circuit/#_circuit-programmation-anchor

[5] Familles en Affaires, HEC Montréal, 2021, [Online], URL address :
https://famillesenaffaires.hec.ca/

bring me, I embarked on the adventure, sure of my decision. Realizing how lucky I had been to have access to this program and the considerable amount of family businesses that exist all over the world, I saw this as a chance to help all those who suffer from the doubts and anxieties that inhabited me a few months ago.

This book is a way for me to thank all the people who have accompanied me in this process by giving back. I have tried to include as much information and examples as possible to allow you to better understand the environment of a family business. The book is divided into three main parts that will serve as steps in your decision-making process: the company, the family and you. The goal is to get you to ask yourself the right questions in a logical order and to guide you in your reflection.

First of all, let me tell you my story. My father is the founder of the family business and the only one who got involved in the company in the first place. My parents had three children: my two older twin brothers and me, much later. My mother and father were 26 and 34 years old, respectively, when my brothers were born. At the time, my father worked for the Mars group in the dog and cat food division, which led him to move every two years. This pace of life was very heavy for the family, and my father, feeling that he had gone around his experience at the Mars group, decided to go into business. It was in 2004 that he created his agri-food distribution company specializing in sweet snacks, cookies and industrial cakes. After 10 years of moving around, this decision allowed my family to settle permanently in one place and that's when my parents decided to have another child: me.

I was born 13 years after my brothers, when my parents were 39 and 47 years old. The big age difference I have with my brothers and parents has pros and cons in developing my father's business takeover plan. The biggest challenge I'm facing right now is the age difference between my parents and me. At 22, I have just finished my studies while my father, who has just celebrated his 70th birthday, is still not retired. So we don't have 10 years ahead of us to prepare for the next generation. All steps must be done quickly and well.

Another challenge I will have to face in the near future is reconciling my personal and professional ambitions. My personal ambition is to live in

Canada; I've been living there since high school and all my friends are there. Currently, my family and the company are the only aspects that connect me

to France. That said, these are not negligible aspects since my wish is to take over the company. I can travel often to see my family, but I would have to be there permanently to take on the day-to-day tasks of the company. Recently, one of my brothers is exploring the idea of joining the family business. We are therefore currently working on paper, to define the different options available to us regarding the sharing of day-to-day management and ownership. As I write this, we have not yet found a miracle solution, although we do have leads that will need to be tested in the coming years.

We will also have decisions to review regarding the property, if my brother decides to join the company with me. Are we going to buy back the shares of our brother who isn't involved? How will we share ownership?

In any case, I remain convinced that I will find a solution to combine my personal and professional ambitions. And who knows? Maybe this challenge will inspire me for a second book!

In the meantime, I hope that this guide will provide you with the necessary tools for your reflection and that it will lead you to flourish in your projects, within the family business or not. My goal is also to make you aware that you are part of a community of people who experience the same thing as you, so that you can share and evolve with those who understand your reality and the daily challenges you face. Taking over a family business is not just a professional project: it's a life project that involves you and your family in a long and difficult process, but so beautiful that it's well worth the effort. So, are you ready to get started?

Step 1:

The company

Chapter 1
The company's activities

Do you really know the activity of your family business? The type of business or industry in which it operates? All the products and services it offers? How many employees does it have? Learning about the company's business is a good starting point to learn more about its overall environment and make an informed decision about your involvement in it.

Its products and services

Can you name at least one product or service that the company offers? If the answer is yes, you can probably name several later. Write them down! You can always check on the company's website all the activities it offers. And if you don't have access to a website, keep this list aside for the preliminary discussion to your integration*. Keep in mind that even if the company sells mostly products, it can also sell services without clearly mentioning them. Negotiation, for example, is a service that can be included directly in the sale price without it appearing on an invoice. Write down everything you can identify as a product or service, as these are part of a process that can be analyzed, improved, and optimized, which is an interesting aspect for you to address when you integrate.

> *** Definition – Integration**: Learning and socialization phase of the new generation in the family business.

Whether you have successfully named one or more products or services offered by the family business, you should be able to determine the industry in which it operates.

Can you accurately determine which industry your company ranks in? Food? Construction? Cosmetics? Electronics? Energy? Equipment? Machining? There are many more. Maybe your business is operating in many of these industries. If your company manufactures construction tools, it operates in the equipment manufacturing industry, but also in mechanics, machining and metal. Let's imagine that your company also offers a tool rental service in parallel. If you have a materials engineering degree, perhaps the "equipment manufacturing, mechanical, machining and metal" part will interest you more and match your skills better than the management part. If, on the contrary, you have a degree in management or are passionate about the field, perhaps you will prefer to start working in the tool rental service. Knowing the industry allows you to get an idea of how you can get involved in the company, beyond the products and services it offers. There are also different ways to sell a product or service in the same industry. Perhaps the way in which the product or service is currently operated isn't optimal and there is room for improvement. You can compare with other companies that aren't necessarily your competitors, but that work in the same field. If you don't know the industry in which your business operates, check out the website or ask a family member who works there. If you don't like the industry, be careful not to stop at this detail! It's quite possible not to feel a strong attachment to the industry in which we work, but to be passionate about our daily tasks since they will not necessarily imply that were in direct contact with the industry, its products or services. The time spent on a product or service that already exists (example: the sale of a toolbox) is minimal. A management job will rather approach the product or service on the surface and your objective will be above all to find ways to sell it. Your proximity to the product should not be a determining factor in your decision to join the family business. Remember that the goal of this exercise is above all to better understand your environment in order to make an informed decision.

It's size

How big is the family business? The stakes are obviously different if it's a start-up than if it's an SME or a large company. If one of your parents has just launched a business and it's still in the start-up stage, you may want to be part of the adventure and help your parents develop the business. There are probably few people already involved in the business and everything is still to be built. By getting involved from the start, you will experience a smoother integration process. The stakes are high because everything is still to be done and you never know if the business will be successful or not. That said, you will have an advantage at the time of your integration and, later, your transition*, since you will be a partner and one of the founders, and you will therefore already have a certain legitimacy within the company.

> *** Definition - Transition**: Corresponds to the transfer of the family business from the outgoing generation to the incoming generation.

In an SME (small or medium-sized enterprise), the stakes of your integration are a little higher. Several generations of the same family have probably been at the helm of the company, so the transition from a parent to a child is part of the culture, unless it's a first experience. In that case, you'll need to do the integration. Either way, you have to prove yourself as "legitimate" before gaining acceptance from employees, which is a daunting but achievable challenge. The advantage of an SME over a large company is that you will move up the ladder more quickly and you will have quickly covered all the departments. Indeed, in large companies, even if the integration process remains similar, the stakes are much higher. The management team (a concept we will discuss later) is probably not only composed of your family, but also of external shareholders who also have veto rights over your desire to join the company. In addition, you probably won't be able to go through all the departments before starting the transition. Some of the employees may therefore be reluctant, if they do not know you, to give you their trust.

As you can probably guess, the size of the company will necessarily influence the way you join it. Your integration strategy will greatly depend on it, which is why it's important to find out about it before you start.

There are three types of companies, but we will only discuss two of them here:

- Private for-profit companies (e.g. SMEs, large companies)
- Private non-profit companies (companies, cooperatives, associations and mutual companies in the social economy[6])

Most family businesses fall into the category of private, for-profit businesses, meaning that they are in majority or wholly owned by corporate entities and are intended to make a profit. Some of you may have a private, not-for-profit business (which is not profit-oriented.) In any case, it's important to know the nature of the business, as it will greatly influence your work internally and your development strategies will therefore be different. Don't go into a business that's completely contrary to your principles or values.

You may also want to look at the company's legal status, which is a valuable source of information about its constitution, shareholders, obligations and rights towards the company. With this information, you will gain a better understanding of the internal environment, but more importantly, of the external environment. Armed with better knowledge of your rights and obligations as a company, you'll be able to better anticipate the next steps in your succession, beyond your integration. You'll be able to move further into the transition and establish several scenarios for your successors. If the company evolves and changes activity or if the number of shareholder-managers changes, this may involve a change in legal status.

With a more detailed view of the external and internal environments of the company, you're now in a position to establish several possible scenarios for your integration and, later, your transition. So ask yourself: is any of this possible for your family and your company? Do any of these scenarios motivate you to join the company?

Depending on the country in which your business is located, the legal status of the company differs. In Quebec, for example, there are three legal forms:

---

[6] Québec, *Démarrer votre entreprise*, Registraire des entreprises Québec, 2017, [Online], URL address :
http://www.registreentreprises.gouv.qc.ca/fr/demarrer/constituer-pmsbl.aspx

sole proprietorship, corporation and partnership.

Here are some of their characteristics.

	Partner(s)	Manager(s)
Sole proprietorship	The sole proprietor	The sole proprietor
Joint stock company	At least one natural or legal person	Shareholders
General partnership	At least 2 natural or legal persons	One or more managers (natural or legal persons)

In France, however, there are additional nuances that are taken into account in the development of the legal status of the company, which multiplies the number of possible legal forms. You can consult a summary table in the appendix.

Chapter 2
The values of the business

Now that you have an overall view of the business, you need to analyze the core of your family business. You will need to assess the values, goals and strategy that guide the management and employees in their day-to-day work and decision making. First, check to see if these concepts are clearly articulated.

All businesses, whether family-owned or not, for-profit or not, rely on their values to guide their actions and decisions. Perhaps the values of the family business appear on its website. If so, great; you already have a solid foundation to work from. But sometimes, especially in small business structures, they aren't necessarily written in black and white. This does not mean that they don't exist. Most of the time, they're carried by the founder and the manager, for whom they seem so obvious that he or she doesn't necessarily think about writing them down. That being said, the values do exist and your job is to identify them and put them on paper.

If these values have been known and displayed for generations, it would be interesting to see if they're still followed, if they have been modified or if new values have been added. In this case, the current leader will not be the founder, but a successor. It's therefore possible that the company's values have evolved over time, with each leader adding his or her own personal touch. Your job will therefore be to verify that the actions and the statement are consistent.

However, if no values exist at this time, you'll need to write them down. In either case, whether the values exist on paper or not, the "task" proposed here is similar. In both cases, you'll need to step into the company to communicate with employees and see how they react to different situations that arise on a daily basis. You'll need to observe directly the recurring behaviors of each person in the different work contexts in order to determine A) what the company's values are and B) if these values are being respected by the staff, regardless of their hierarchical level. In addition to observing, you can and should, at some point, communicate with the various people involved in the company. You can ask them, for example, to determine which values they believe the company promotes and which guide each of their daily decisions. In general, they are 3 to 5 values per company, but never more than 6. If you need a method to help you define or redefine your family business values, Jim Collins explains this topic in detail in his book Built to Last - Successful Habits of Visionary Companies[7]. I personally used his online guide[8] to redefine the values of my family business during a meeting with all members of the company, which took place during my integration. Defining and writing the values was one of my first personal projects in my family business and it was very well received by the members once I explained the importance of it. This first action propelled my integration and allowed me to carry out new improvement projects, such as the redesign of the website, but it also showed the whole team that I was attentive to the company's mission and culture (concepts that we will discuss later), which helped reinforce my legitimacy.

If you're already involved or have worked in the family business for a short period of time, such as during school breaks, this exercise on values will be

---

[7] COLLINS, Jim, *Built to Last : Successful Habits of Visionary Companies*, 3e éd., New York, Harper Business, 1994, 368 p.

[8] COLLINS, J., *Vision Framework*, JimCollins.com, 2001, [Online], URL address : https://www.jimcollins.com/tools/vision-framework.pdf

easier for you. You may be able to recall one or more events that were guided by certain values. However, if you can't visit the business right now because of distance or because you don't feel ready to take on this project, don't panic! There's another solution available to you. Since the values of the family business often reflect the founder and his or her past and present leaders, analyze the personal values of your grandparents, parents, aunts or uncles and anyone else you know who has run the business. This will give you a good idea of what the company's values might look like. This may not be as effective as visiting the workplace in person, but you won't be able to determine the values accurately until you're involved on a daily basis, and the purpose of this exercise is primarily to help you analyse the family business environment to get you thinking about your possible fit.

Now that you have a sense of the family business' activities and values, the picture should begin to emerge, as should your opinion. We will then explore the family business a little further to understand its present and future challenges and to help you propel yourself into it. In addition to its values, each company has a mission. This mission is specific to the company, justifies its reason of being, but its main characteristic is that it's unattainable.

Let's take The Walt Disney Company as an example. The original mission of the company was, quite simply, «to make people happy»[9], which was not really achievable since it's impossible to make everyone happy. Today, the mission has changed and is more of a "corporate vision". Indeed, to this day, The Walt Disney Company's mission " is to entertain, inform and inspire people around the globe through the power of unparalleled storytelling, reflecting the iconic brands, creative minds and innovative technologies that make ours the world premier entertainment company." However, it's their original mission that has driven each of their projects in the past and has been the basic argument for their decisions. In more graphic terms, here's how the mission exerts its directional power:

---

[9] RASMUS, D. W., Defining your company's Vision, Fast Company, 2012, [Online], URL address: https://www.fastcompany.com/1821021/defining-your-companys-vision

How could we make people happy? → (new project)

What really makes people happy? → (decision making)

So what is the mission of your family business? How will you guide your decisions within it? Again, the mission may not be written in black and white although it exists. You will need to state it. If necessary, refer again to Jim Collins' work cited above. There you'll find questions to guide your thinking and methods for thinking as a team.

Now that you know a little more about the business and "personality" of your company, you can more or less determine where the company will be in two or three decades. In the same vein, in addition to the values and mission, you should also determine a long-term goal for the next 25 to 30 years. In this case, make sure that this goal is actually achievable. At this stage, you can also use Jim Collins' method to determine, with the other members involved, the long-term goal.

As before, if your thinking is completely personal at this point, you can still do the exercise with the research you've done since you started reading. If you're still missing too much information, determine a goal that you would like to pursue if you were to join the company. Keep in mind that it's very important to determine one before you start, or at least before you join. Since this goal will guide your integration through the re-entry phase* and beyond, make sure that this goal inspires and motivates you for the next 25 to 30 years. Even if you can't anticipate it completely, by identifying short-term and long-term strategies, you'll be able to break the goal down into parts that correspond roughly to each stage of your integration, right up to succession. By breaking down the goal into several strategies, you'll also see whether or not all of these steps "speak" to you. If this motivates you, great! It's one step closer to becoming part of the family business. If it doesn't motivate you at all, perhaps you should consider another goal.

> ***Definition - Repreneurship**: The act of taking over or buying an existing business.

Be careful, however, not to confuse "apprehension" with "disinterest". It's normal to be afraid of a project of this scope, spread over several years. However, breaking it down into several strategies will make it less overwhelming. Also, remember that you will probably not be doing it alone. A long-term goal is a collective effort in which all departments will participate in some way. So the question to ask yourself is: how will you participate in this collective effort in your daily work? If this question inspires you more than the goal itself, you're on the right track. We'll talk more about the goal itself and what it will do for you professionally or personally.

Chapter 3
The gouvernance of the family business

The 3 circles Model

Before we dive into the definition of governance and what constitutes it, we need to discuss a very instructive model that will help you understand how the family business is constructed. The 3 circles model[10] represents the delicate balance between the 3 spheres that make up a family business. There is family, business and ownership. These spheres represent systems made up of people and orchestrated by different boards. It's at the heart of these three circles that we find the different governance systems.

---

[10] DAVIS, J., TAGIURI, R., *The Influence of Life Stages on Father-Son Work Relationships in Family Companies*, Unpublished manuscript, Graduate School of Business Administration, University of Southern California, 1982, 924 p.

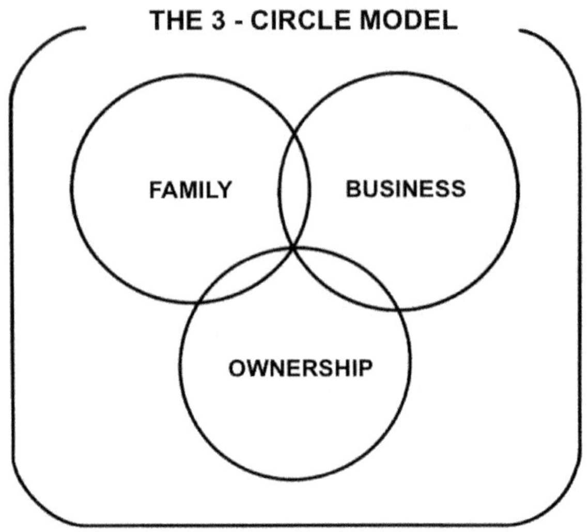

TAGIURI AND DAVIS, 1982

Governance is "the set of forums governing the information, decision-making and monitoring processes"[11]. Thus, in the context of family businesses, governance can be defined as "a system of processes and structures put in place at the highest level of the company, the family and the shareholders, to ensure the best decisions regarding the direction, responsibilities and control of the company". [12] Just as an ordinary company has governance systems at the corporate and shareholder level, the family business has these same systems to which the family is added as part of the overall balance. This structure ensures, among other things, that objectives are followed, that

---

[11] Circuit – Sur la voie de la relève, « La gouvernance », [notes taken as part of the Le Circuit program], HEC Montréal, Montréal, February 2020

[12] KENYON-ROUVINEZ, D., WARD, J. L., *L'importance de la gouvernance familiale et de la gouvernance entrepreneuriale*, dans *Les entreprises familiales*, Presses Universitaires de France, 2004, 127 p.

communication is good and that decisions are made in a democratic way.

Each circle and zone has different issues and systems. The goal of governance is therefore to orchestrate these systems to ensure the sustainability of the company, which isn't as simple as one might imagine.

THE 7 TERRITORIES

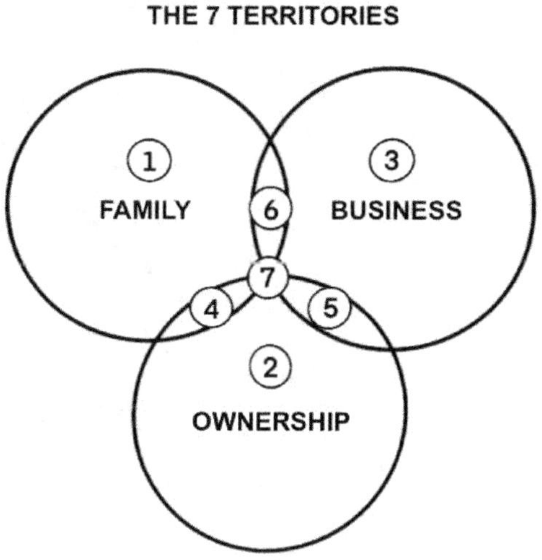

In the diagram above, each number represents a territory. There are seven of them. These territories are composed of people, all direct or indirect actors of the family business. Let's analyze some of them.

Number 1 simply represents the family members. They're not shareholders (they don't own property) and aren't involved in the business. Number 2 represents people who own property (shareholders) but are neither part of the family nor involved in the business as employees. Number 3, represents employees who are not family members. In zone 4, we find, for example, family members who own shares in the company, but are not employees. Finally, number 7 often represents the president of the company (one or both of your parents) who is therefore a family member who works in the company on a daily basis and holds title to the company.

As an example, here is the 3-circle model adapted to my situation:

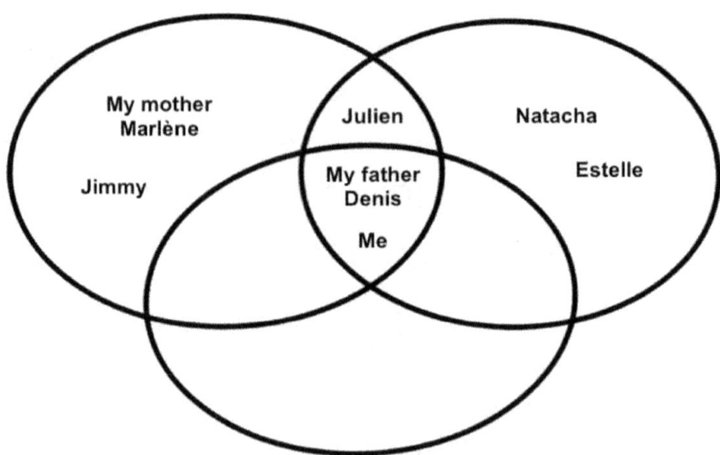

These systems are not complex, but governance is essential for the proper management of the company and its various stakeholders.

Governance structures[13]

Let's now look at the different governance systems provided for each circle. We will review each of them in order to study their respective roles in the overall governance of the company.

---

[13] CISNEROS, L., *La Gouvernance*, Circuit – Sur la voie de la relève, PowerPoint presentation, HEC Montréal, 2020

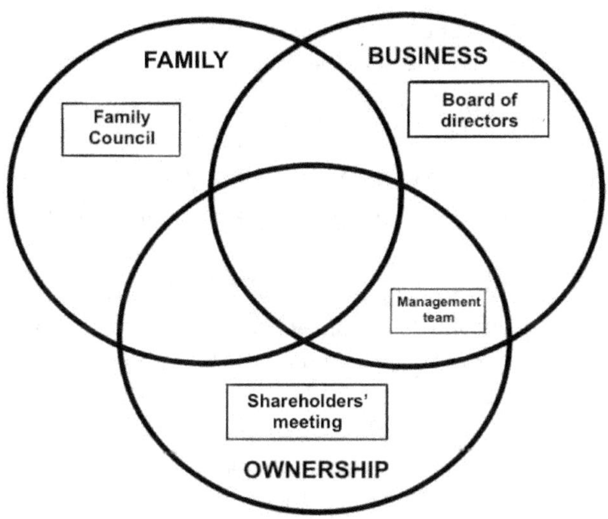

A) The family council

The family council is a governance structure that brings together only the members of the family, sometimes extended, whether or not they're involved in the business. The council is "the communication forum of the family. It allows family members to talk about their personal and professional aspirations, to discuss the family's involvement in the business, and to initiate discussions on plans for the continuity of the family's assets"[14]. This council promotes exchange and communication between involved and uninvolved members. The council also makes it possible to make decisions regarding members (hiring or firing) and to resolve conflicts. Its main functions, according to Beaucage and Paré Julien (2020), are:

-   Establish the family code of conduct
-   Develop family vision, mission and commitments
-   Develop and implement family policies

---

[14] BEAUCAGE, C., PARÉ-JULIEN, D., *Le petit guide de la famille en affaires – Le conseil de famille*, Éditions JFD, Montréal, 2020, 40 p.

- Anticipate and resolve problems between family members (with each other and with the company)
- Managing conflict between family members
- Implementing elements of family governance
- Promote family values and vision
- Plan and organize family activities, events and meetings
- Fostering a climate of respect, trust and affection within the family
- Promote the concept of mentoring and planning for family members' career goals
- Manage family and family member related tasks (training, education, mentoring, philanthropy, family financial investment, etc.)
- Preparing the next generation to join the company

Setting up such council is not easy; it requires getting the whole family to accept the concept. Note that it's strongly recommended to be accompanied by a professional in the setting up of the board and the first meetings.

B) The Board of Directors

In a family business, the board of directors is the link between the family and the management of the business. The board of directors is "composed, for the most part, of competent, independent members from outside the family in order to be able to carry out this responsibility with professionalism, objectivity (without emotion) and to be able to give good advice, especially when the company is smaller and doesn't have all the skills"[15]. The members of the board of directors are often independent contractors with family and managers who work in the company (3). Some of these managers may still be part of the family (6) or be shareholders and part of the management team (5). The main functions are[16]:

---

[15] Circuit – Sur la voie de la relève, « La gouvernance », [notes taken as part of the Le Circuit program], HEC Montréal, Montréal, February 2020

[16] Circuit – Sur la voie de la relève, « La gouvernance », [notes taken as part of the Le Circuit program], HEC Montréal, Montréal, February 2020

- Evaluating the CEO
- Monitoring the performance of the company
- Provide support and advice to the management team
- Provide input into and approve the strategic planning process
- Mentoring family members who are employed in the business and advising on maintaining harmonious family relationships
- Approve the appointment of the management team
- Monitor financial and legal matters
- Act as a liaison between the family shareholders and the management team

C) The shareholders' meeting

The shareholders' meeting, also known as the "partners' council", is a forum for reflection, orientation and decision-making that has an impact on the investments made or to be made. Remember, shareholders can be family members without being involved in the business (4) they can be external to the family while being involved in the business (5) or they can simply be shareholders and not be part of the family or the business (2).

The main functions of the shareholders' meeting are similar to those of an ordinary company[17]:

- Resource allocation
- Monitoring the return on investment
- Deciding on the distribution of dividends
- Selling and buying back shares
- Implementing the shareholders' agreement

Because governance systems are quite technical and theoretical, they're often difficult to implement in real life. In fact, you may not have any of these tips in your companies right now. Keep them in mind, as these tips are often

---

[17] Circuit – Sur la voie de la relève, « La gouvernance », [notes taken as part of the Le Circuit program], HEC Montréal, Montréal, February 2020

a must during the transition process from one generation to the next. Good communication is key to a successful integration and transition, hence the need to set up several councils bringing together the different stakeholders of the company, according to their concerns and responsibilities within the company. With the support of a professional, the different governance systems will be put in place little by little to match the issues and the personality of the company.

Political skills[18]

Political skills are skills that allow a person to gain influence. They can be very useful when it comes to holding a position in the family business. However, be careful not to mix influence with manipulation! When you influence, you want to help or advance a person, whereas when you manipulate, your intentions may be harmful. Keep in mind your ultimate goal when using this skill: political skills must allow you to be recognized as a person who helps others to advance and progress. This is a skill that is learned slowly, but surely. In this case, the advantage of the family business is that you can use your circle of influence to develop this skill. To help you see things more clearly, let's look at some strategies that you can put in place as soon as you join the family business.

1. Use your power levers

There are two types of power: formal power and informal power. As the name implies, formal power is acquired through the position or title a person has in the company. Since you're probably not going to take over as president overnight, you'll need to use informal power to make your mark. Informal power is recognized by the skills, expertise or information you have about your environment and the charisma you exude. It may seem like a big job to do at the beginning of your business, but developing political skills takes time. Just think about how long it would take you to reach a position or office that would give you formal power; it will probably take as long or longer to hold informal power. You're never finished learning, so you will never fully master

---

[18] LAINEY, P., *Les habiletés politique*, Circuit – Sur la voie de la relève, PowerPoint presentation, HEC Montréal, 2020

all the elements that make up informal power, but it's by honing your skills a little more each day, with the people around you, that you'll eventually achieve it. By acquiring these skills, you'll also carve out a place for yourself within the family business.

Here are some questions you can answer to gauge where you stand on your political skills:

Your formal power:

- What does your current position in the company allow you to do?
- What does your current position in the company don't allow you to do?

Your informal power:

- What acquired knowledge do you have that gives you credibility?
- What experiences, professional or otherwise, give you credibility?
- Identify the key influencers in your family business (note that these key players can be both inside and outside the business).
- Ask 3 people to tell you how they feel in your presence. Identify recurring elements and try to think of how these elements can become levers of power.

2. Analyze and leverage your environment

To determine who has power or influence in the business right now, you need to analyze your environment. These people can be strong allies when you enter the family business. If one of your parents is in charge of the company, he or she will be able to confirm your skills and justify your presence in the company by solid arguments rather than by the simple fact that you're their son or daughter. Of course, you'll still have to prove yourself, but by having the support of management, you will have a head start. However, it's always tricky to come into the business with your parents behind you. So if possible, try to find other influential allies.

Determining your internal circle of influence can also be a great advantage if you decide to take over the company, since you will already have people on your side to support your skills in front of the administration. Once in the company, don't neglect this analysis phase.

- Observe who is making decisions and who is making "business happen"
- Observe each other's behaviors
- Recognize who is often called upon and who is usually asked for advice
- Identify who has influence over those you wish to influence. For example, who has influence over your parents (or company executives)?
- Keep in mind that influencers may also be outside your family business, in the family circle or the shareholder circle, for example. To help you identify the influential people in your environment, you can map it
- Identify the people you need to influence to move your project forward
- Highlight in yellow those who have formal power
- Highlight in pink those who have informal power
- Frame those with whom you already have a strong, direct and positive relationship. They will potentially be your first allies. Try to think about the interests of each of the actors in your environment

3. Create alliances and share your power

Now that you've developed your political skills and know the influential people around you, why not create alliances to join forces? Your skills, expertise and information can most likely help someone on a project, for example, and in return, it helps you make your mark independently of your parents.

Remember to do things ethically; otherwise you'll fall into manipulation and risk tarnishing your image with others. To help you stay on track, ask yourself these questions:

- Am I acting in the collective interest of the family and the company?
- Do I act in accordance with the laws and regulations?
- Am I acting in accordance with my morals and values?

If you are still on the right track, great! Now let's look at how you can create alliances:

- Look at the mapping you just did. Do you see potential alliances and collaborations?
- What are your goals and interests for each of these potential alliances?
- Are your goals and interests aligned with those of the identified stakeholders?

4.   Recognize the people around you

Showing recognition makes people more willing to collaborate: it's the fuel of motivation! Recognizing the accomplishments of previous generations and taking the time to acknowledge and thank them can make a big difference in establishing your influence in the company. Being grateful is an excellent lever of power.

If you have ideas in your head to improve the company, that's great! Keep them and be prepared to present them to management, whether they're your parents or not. But be careful how you present your plans! Always keep in mind that you owe some respect to previous generations and the current generation. They may have some gaps, such as digital marketing or information technology. Still, take the trouble to acknowledge their knowledge and expertise, which they have acquired over the years and which has contributed to the company's success.

Even if you think you have a lot to teach them (and you may), they also have a lot to teach you from their past successes and mistakes. That's the wealth in family business. You have the chance to be in constant contact with entire generations who have been learning your future business for years. . It's true that the world is constantly changing and that there will always be things to improve or change, or that previous generations won't have experienced. But that doesn't make them any less credible. Acknowledge their strengths and weaknesses and move forward together by feeding each other's knowledge. Never think that you can teach them their job, it will only damage your relationship.

Step 2:

The Family

Chapter 4
Family Environment Analysis

The composition

Before analyzing the family business, you'll need to know the entire family. Remember the 3-circle model: in the family circle, the entire family is shown whether or not they're involved in the business. Be careful, though! When we talk about "complete family", we are referring only to close family members. If your family business involves only your parents and siblings, there's no need to include your aunts and uncles in the circle, unless they can be closely linked to your immediate family's decision making, for example, if your parents have guardianship of your cousin. Otherwise, focus only on your immediate family members.

For me, since my father, brother and I work in the company, I will only include my second brother and mother in the circle. Later on, I may also include my spouse and children.

Now, let's talk a bit about the importance of including family members who aren't involved in the family business in the circle. First, these members are often considered when making internal business decisions. Whether we do it consciously or not, we necessarily think of our immediate family when we make a business decision, especially in a family business. Think about it for a moment. If you were an employee of a company you didn't own and your boss offered you a transfer across the country, you would probably consult your spouse before accepting. The same is true in a family business. You'll need to consider your immediate family when making long-term decisions. This can include more than just your parents and siblings! If your aunts and uncles are involved in the business, chances are your cousins will also join if they haven't already. In this case, their spouses and children should also be included in the family circle. Even though these members may seem distant, the business binds you and requires that they be considered.

Now it's your turn!

Write on the left the first names of the people in your family (by marriage or blood) who aren't in the business, and on the right, the first names of the people in your family who are involved in the business (at all levels).

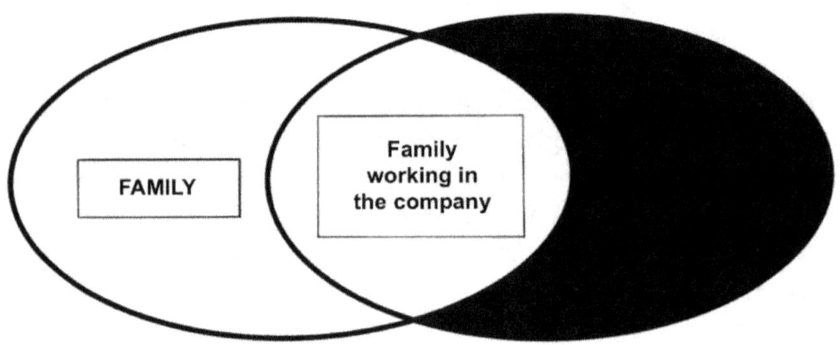

Relations

Now that you have listed the active family members who are in the business and the close family members who aren't involved, you'll need to look at the relationships between all these people. When we talk about relationships, were referring primarily to conflicts and alliances. Since your family is part of your business environment, studying the different relationships within it will be very important in order to determine your political strategy and to avoid getting involved in conflicts unintentionally. For this, we will use a tool called the genogram[19].

---

[19] WHITESIDE, M., ARONOFF, C., WARD, J., *How families work together*, 2e éd.,

It's actually a family tree that also deals with the relationships between people in the same family. If your family business is older, you can go as far back as the founder to start your tree and look at all the relationships in your family, past and present. If your family business was started by one of your parents, it may not be necessary to go back any further; it's up to you. The purpose of this exercise is to understand the current environment of the family business through the family's relationships. This way, you'll be able to avoid conflicting relationships and foster fulfilling relationships in the family and in the business, while identifying life events that may affect family functioning. You'll also be able to anticipate these events to avoid conflict and see if there are repetitive patterns across generations. By studying the patterns, you'll be better prepared for conflicts that may arise.

It's your turn! Build your own genogram using the symbols in the following diagrams. They will help you to know how to identify each family member and correctly mark the links between them.

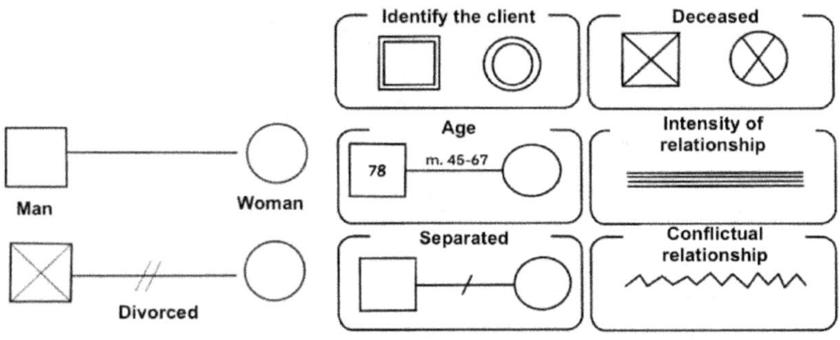

Family Business Consulting Group Publications, New York, 1993, 99 p.

As an example, here's the genogram adapted to my situation:

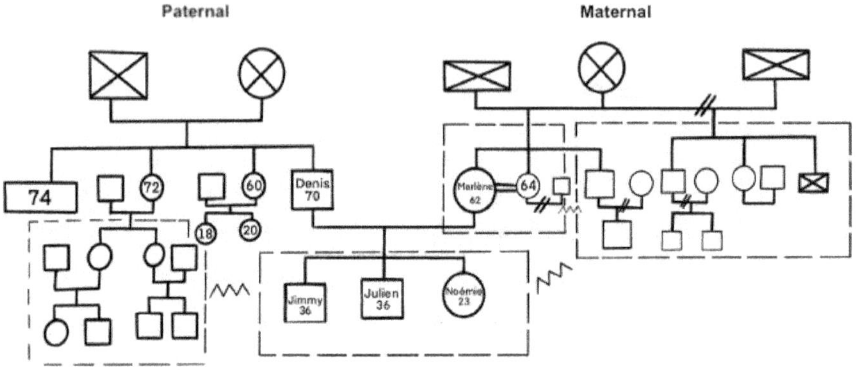

Paternal   Maternal

74   72   60   Denis 70   Marlène 62   64   18   20   Jimmy 36   Julien 36   Noémie 23

Note that even though the genogram is a theoretical tool, it can, at best, reveal trends, but it can't predict the behavior of individuals. It's also possible that you may be wrong. Since you're analyzing your family's relationships, you may not have all the information you need about a situation and, as a result, you may think that old conflicts still exist when they were resolved many years ago. The people involved may have naturally become more distant as a result of their conflict. Also, if you go back in time, you may miss some information.

If you weren't born or were a child, you may not have all the details of the story to fully analyze the situation. However, this can be a good opportunity to talk to your parents or trusted family members about various conflicts that have occurred in the family, past or present. Remember, communication is key to resolving these types of issues! This can also be an opportunity to resolve existing conflicts between you and a family member. Especially if you're preparing to work together in the future, it may be time to revisit some of the issues to move forward.

Most conflicts are also the result of misinterpretation, and if you've let some time pass since that conflict, water has probably passed under the bridge and you're probably able to explain yourself more calmly. If you feel uncomfortable confronting this person, don't hesitate to use a mediator. Whether it's someone from outside the family or someone you know is neutral, make sure they can keep the tone down and ask the right questions to resolve the conflict. If the conflict is larger and involves more than one person in the family, you may also want to call for a special family council.

Conflicts between people and especially within families are natural and healthy, but staying on bad terms and letting relationships deteriorate or become toxic isn't desirable and must be addressed before it damages the people involved and those around them. No one likes to see a family torn apart, and when it comes to a business family, the stakes are higher as conflicts can affect the business and spill over to employees outside the family. So remember that relationships are bound to change over time. You have represented here the genogram of your family currently in business, but you'll surely have to redo one eventually to represent new alliances (marriages), new people (spouse and children), deaths, etc. I suggest that you keep this tool handy. Relationships, whether they're characterized by alliances or conflicts, tend to intensify over the generations. Imagine the picture: your parents started out alone (two), they may have had three children (counting you). If each child has three children of his own, that's nine grandchildren who may someday become involved in the family business. It's unlikely that all nine will want to join the business, but it's not impossible. One day, those nine grandchildren will have spouses and children of their own. As the number of family members involved in the business grows, so does the potential for conflict. Especially if several people want to take over the business...

Chapter 5
The Family in the Business

Today

Do you know who runs the business today? Is it one person or is there more than one person running the business? Does the same person own all the titles of ownership or are they shared among the different managers?

Before you get into the family business, you need to know the issues surrounding its management and ownership, especially if you ever want to take it over. Let's start at the beginning. Who is currently running the family business? Is it your grandfather or grandmother? Your father or mother? Your aunt, uncle, brother or sister? In my case, the leader is my father, which means that he's in charge of the moral, financial and legal aspects of the business and is responsible to determine the short, medium and long term strategies. He has the official title of CEO and is the sole Director.

So who runs your family business and how much of it does that person own? Is this person alone or does he or she share the Manager title with another person? Is this other person part of the family or an outsider? The same titles are often used in different businesses, but they don't always mean the same thing. Beyond the title of president, you should be interested in the role of the leader with respect to the company as a whole, but more importantly with respect to the employees (family and non-family) and their daily tasks. You don't have to know right away if you want to take over the family business to look at what makes it tick. I would advise you to look into it anyway!

Beyond the fact that anyone who works in a company needs to know how it's run, you probably have the responsibility, even if it's not your goal yet, to take over the company the day the Manager retires. Of course, you can refuse if you don't want to, but you should know that, in your parents' minds, you have probably been in the running since you were born. In your case, it's even more important to have the management structure in mind if you finally decide to embark on the succession process or if an accident happens before you begin the process. No one is immune to accidents, especially as the leaders, usually your grandparents or parents age. You probably don't want to think about it, let alone discuss it. Yet this conversation is imperative. Do you know who is responsible for taking over the business in the event of an accident or the death of the Manager? If you're on the list of potential successors, you'd probably like to know. And even if taking over the business is your ultimate goal, your ideal scenario is certainly not to take over literally overnight!

The reason succession planning is called a process is because it's made up of several steps to ensure your training. And even if you're prepared, between the emotional shock of an accident or the loss of a loved one and the new responsibilities you'll be entrusted with, it can be very easy to lose your footing.

Let's look at a concrete example:

Your parents go skiing and your father, who is the leader, breaks his leg. He has to undergo surgery and be off work for a week. He's mentally fit and able to perform certain tasks within the company, but he needs someone to be there to keep things running smoothly and he puts you in charge temporarily. What do you do? Are you able to help him/her for a week to keep the business running smoothly during his/her absence? Will you be willing to talk to the right people to delegate certain tasks, to make sure that the payments for the week are made? In short, it's essential that you know how the company and its management operate outside of your personal and professional goals. You must be prepared for any eventuality.

Family businesses have this particularity: even if you're just starting out and it's a small business, you could be asked to replace the boss at a moment's notice if needed. Knowing your environment will greatly assist you in performing your duties should you be asked to manage the business for a temporary period.

Now that you know who runs the business, do you know who owns it? Is the business owned by the person or people who run it? Is the business owned exclusively by family members, or do outsiders also own shares? Ownership of a business is defined by percentage shares. These shares are calculated according to the contribution of an individual to the company in relation to its capital. Thus, one person, often the founder, may have 100% ownership of the business. In a family business, the owner may decide to "give" shares to his or her children, the next generation, to facilitate the transfer. My father, for example, "gave" 10% to each of my brothers while he gave me 20%. This difference is explained by the age difference between my brothers and me. When my brother and I are a little further along in our project, we will re-evaluate the purchase of our brother's shares and our father's shares.

Property titles are part of the field of finance and not the subject of this book. So I won't go into that. The point of this section is simply to show you that there are many nuances to running a business, especially in the case of a family business. The subject is quite complex and each family and business has its own particularities. By the end of this chapter, you should have a clearer idea of what makes up management and a better understanding of what ownership is in general. You'll be more aware of your environment and will be able to make decisions that affect you in the way you want to. Before you finish this section, go back to your 3-circle model and re-fill in the ownership circle and the parts in between that intersect with the business and family.

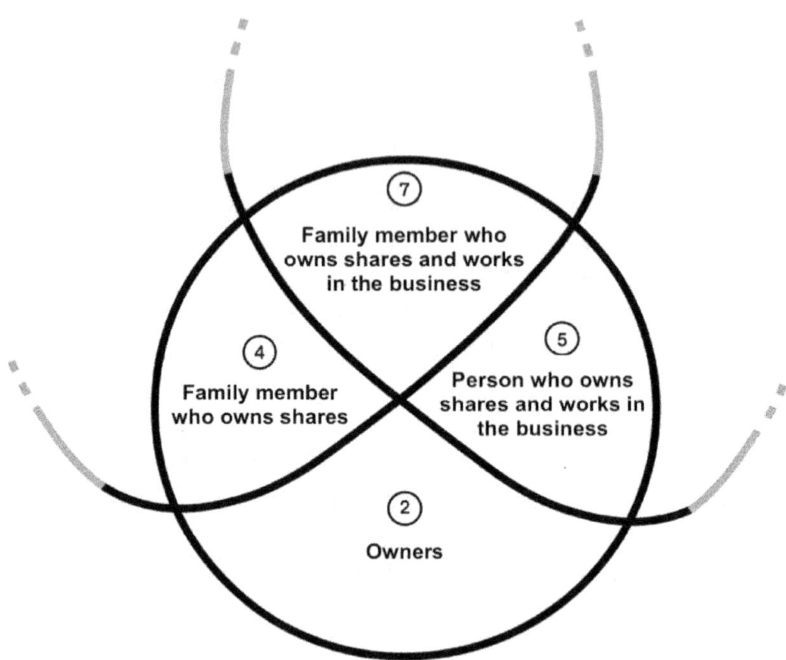

Did you get it right the first time or did you have to add, change or remove people? As you can see, this model is evolutionary, first in terms of the movement of people, but also in your understanding of the business environment. Keep this tool handy as you read we will use it a few times.

Tomorrow

Who's the next generation? And what will the family business structure look like after succession? Now that you have a clear understanding of the current environment, it's time to imagine what your future would look like if you decided to get involved in the family business. There's no need to play psychic; effective communication with your family members will be enough to enlighten you.

As you talk with those around you, see who seems to want to get involved and who seems to want to take over the family business. As you can see, not every discussion you undertake now is decisive. It's not about asking the person in front of you to decide the rest of his or her life right now. These discussions are simply intended to initiate a process of reflection on succession that can be explored again and again before and during the process. People can change their minds very quickly and without notice, so it's important to check in regularly with everyone's thoughts and decisions. While writing this book, one of my brothers announced that he was considering joining the family business. As I write this, he's on probation. At 36 years old, he has already held various positions in several companies, so it's never too late to try!

Many people may want to do something, such as take over the business, but realize along the way how much work goes into it, only to become discouraged and lose interest. It's natural and normal to change your mind, even if this frequent back-and-forth can be annoying over time. Keep it cool and try to be supportive of the person who needs it. They are probably experiencing uncertainty or fear about taking on such an important project, as you may be if you're reading this book right now. You may be wondering whether to get involved in the family business or to take over from the current generation, and you've probably changed your mind many times over the pages! Be patient with yourself and especially with your family; after all, a succession process can take 10 years! In such an important personal and professional project, you want to give yourself the means to succeed and since your family is directly affected by your decision, you probably don't want to waste their time and disappoint them.

As such, the succession landscape is bound to change in the years leading up to, and even during, its implementation. The analysis you do today will most likely change by then, but starting now will help you in your decision-making process. For this projection exercise, go back to your 3-circle model. This time, use the 3 circles as in Chapter 2 of this book and project yourself 10 years into the future.

THE 7 TERRITORIES

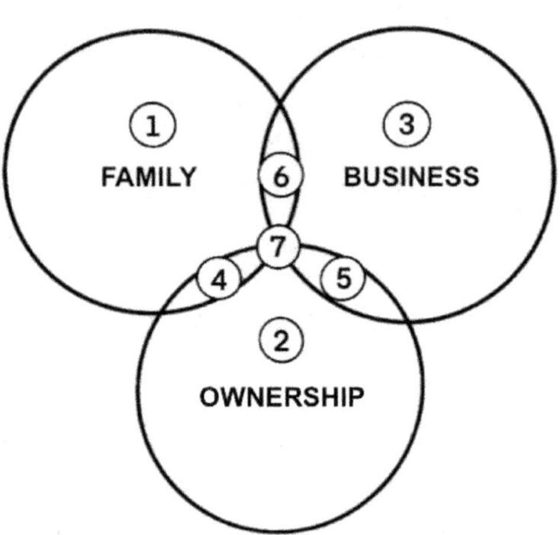

Let's start with the family circle (1 and 6). How old are your parents, brothers and sisters right now? How old are you? If you can, keep this information somewhere. Estimating the ages of your family members in 10 years will allow you to estimate the time remaining before succession and to build a plan of action accordingly. How old will your brothers and sisters be in 10 years? If they're still young today, will they be old enough to say whether they want to be involved in the family business? Or are they older than you and planning to start a family? Perhaps they will be satisfied with their own career plans and won't want to get involved; the scenarios are many! If you think they will have children, add them to Family Zone 1. Remember, close family influences the behavior of those around you! And consider moving your siblings into Zone 6, the middle zone between family and business, if you think they will be involved in the business. We'll explore the nuances later.

These questions are difficult, and almost impossible to answer with certainty, but remember that this is a projection exercise that's intended to help you visualize your future in the family business. What about you? How old will you be in 10 years? Where do you see yourself? Does your vision match your current decisions? Can you imagine yourself in a different company or in a different position than in the family business? What is your personal life like? Do you have children? You can put all of these assumptions in the family circle, right on your model. Finally, do you place yourself in Family Zone 1 or Zone 6 with one foot in the business? How old will your parents be? If you expect your parents to be retired, put them in Zone 1, the family, since they will no longer be officially involved.

Let's continue with the company circle. Using the same model, try to estimate the movement of employees over the next 10 years. Obviously, in the case of a SME with a dozen employees, this work is much simpler than for a multinational. If your company has a lot of employees, try to think by sector of activity or by number. For example, are there certain sectors that are likely to disappear due to the evolution of technology, or is the number of employees likely to increase or decrease?

Again, the goal here is to give you an idea of the evolution of the family business environment. If you decide to take over the management, it's important that you know the number of employees and the different areas of activity that make up the business, especially since you'll probably have to do a tour of the departments during your integration in the field. If your company is smaller and you can get to know each person who works there, the question of retirements and new positions will be more important. Are there employees who will be retiring in the next 10 years, or is there a new project under development that will require more manpower or workers, leading you to hire a number of people?

Now, write down in Zone 3 the people or areas of activity that you expect to keep over the next 10 years. Obviously, we can't anticipate changes in each individual's life (moving, getting married, new job), but the purpose here is simply to give you an idea of who will be working with you or you will manage. Maybe someone you don't like will retire and that will cause you to think about taking over the business.

I won't go into this in depth, but you can also note the movement of people who appear in Zone 5, if there are any. These are people outside the family who are employed in the business and have ownership shares. This is quite rare in family businesses, so I won't elaborate on this aspect, since your general understanding of the subject should be quite good by now.

The last circle is no small one! It concerns the ownership of the family business. Here, several scenarios can be developed. The first is the simplest: one person, you or another family member, such as your brother or sister, takes over the entire property. In a more complex way, it's also possible to take over as a team. Two or more people can also decide to take over the business together and divide the property in this way. Note that it's not mandatory to share equally. If one person has been involved for a much longer period of time, he can have more shares than his partner who has just joined the adventure. Here, we are talking about cases where the family takes over the entire property.

On our 3-circle model, we are therefore at number 4.

Zone 2 represents the external owners of the company. It can happen that for financial reasons, the managers of the family business take the decision to sell part of it to external people. By focusing on zones 4 and 2, we can see at a glance, whether the family business is managed exclusively by the family, shared between the family and external shareholders or only external shareholders, but in this case, we can no longer speak of a family business since the family no longer has most of the ownership.

To close this chapter, tell me: how do you see the ownership of the business in 10 years? Do you think that you'll be the only person involved after your parents, or will other member in your family want to own the business as well? Do you know of any potential successors in your family or do you think your parents will have to sell the business to outside shareholders? If the latter is currently being considered, how does that make you feel? Are you sad or relieved? Do you want to do everything possible to keep the family business "in the family"?

For example, in 10 years, my family's business environment could look like this:

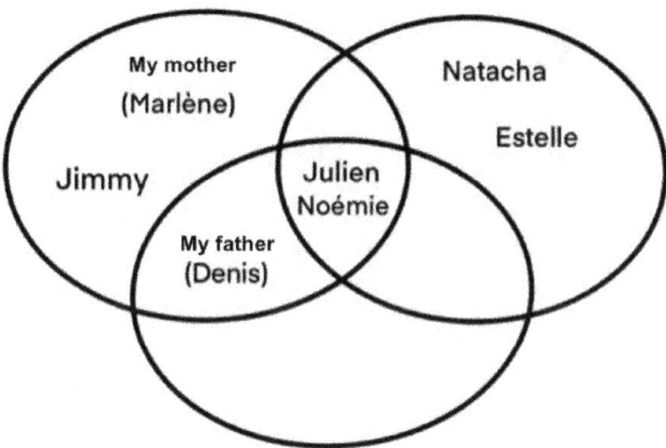

Chapter 6
Legacy

Cultural Capital

When we think of inheritance, we often think of the money and property that we can get back when our parents die. This subject is often considered taboo and a source of conflict for children. But there's another heritage that we don't often talk about and that's much more important than a few material goods left by our parents: the cultural heritage.

The cultural heritage represents mainly the values, principles and traditions that our parents instilled in us from birth and that participate in the development of our personality, but also in the main features that determine and unite our family. This cultural heritage is even more present in a family business. On the one hand, there are family values and on the other hand, the values of the family business. All of them are linked through the family members involved in the business and, more specifically, through the leader.

Family culture and corporate culture are often similar and rarely contradictory, which will make your integration much easier. A company's values, as we saw in Chapter 1, are often a reflection of the founder or leader, and since values are part of a person's personality, it's virtually impossible for their values to be radically opposed between home and office.

In Chapter 1, you identified your company's values. Now you'll repeat the exercise to analyze your family's values. Look at your parents: what values does your mother hold above all others? What are your father's values? What are your family values? Do they represent the values of both your parents? If so, is the mix harmonious or does it cause some friction? Have different values been added to your family with the arrival of new members? What are they? Respect, honesty, autonomy, solidarity?

Keep your notes on company and family values aside, we will look at them again in the last section when you determine your personal values.

Cultural heritage also includes traditions. Family traditions can be passed on through holidays, religion or even food! They often result in situations where the family shares common values of togetherness, empathy and solidarity. Can you think of a few traditions that your family has kept? Is your family religious? Are their traditions related to the practice of a particular religion? For example, do you celebrate Christmas? And if so, in what way?

List some of your family traditions and see if any of them have found their way into the family business. For example, at Christmas, how does your tradition translate into the business? Do you decorate the office with a tree? Is there a special evening? Or a gift exchange? If you can't think of any family traditions the company observes, ask yourself if this is something you would want to implement if you joined the company? Are all your traditions applicable to the corporate world? Do you think that holidays from religious backgrounds could fit into the company and, if so, how could you adapt your family traditions to the diversity of the company?

Most family holidays are based on the family's traditional religion and can be tricky to incorporate into the business world, where beliefs may differ. Be sensitive and don't hesitate to ask for input if you want to share your family traditions in the workplace. By engaging them, you'll have a better chance of success.

Combining family traditions with the family business brings employees and family together to create one big "family" within the business; a family with its own traditions and values, but one that draws on your family's and to which past leaders have added their two cents. By including employees in the larger corporate family, you not only improve their engagement, but you also share the cultural heritage of your ancestors and help them connect to the company. Thus, the culture of a family business, which we discussed in Chapter 1, draws heavily from the family cultural heritage, which is why it's important to analyze your family culture and the company's culture, together and separately, to identify similarities and differences. Keep in mind that you're free to interpret your analyses as you wish. In this area, there's no wrong answer. The purpose is simply to show you the different avenues available to you if you decide to join the family business. You can certainly make a contribution and be an active part of the family legacy in the family business. It's a great way to recognize previous generations, as we mentioned in Chapter 3, and to begin your integration.

Economic capital

The cultural heritage of the family that's incorporated into the business creates a strong emotional attachment. The company becomes, in spite of itself, both a family for the people who work there and a full member of the family for the family in business. Almost like a child, it requires daily attention.

The emotional attachment is even stronger when the management of the company has been passed on for several generations already, a bit like a precious family jewel, and when all its managers and you yourself have been in contact with it in one way or another since you were young. You've probably seen your parents work hard to take care of it as if it were one of their children, and, just as with a family member, no one wants to see the business fail, struggle or disappear. You and your parents may want to keep it in the family in order to preserve the corporate culture. Only a family member can continue the family values and traditions. Since the attachment to the family business is often very strong, it's difficult to consider it as a simple legacy and it's equally difficult for the outgoing generation to part with it. The division of shares in a family business between the outgoing and incoming generations is very delicate and often takes place in several stages specific to each business and family. The purpose of this book isn't to identify the steps in the succession process, but rather to help you identify the issues and encourage you to start conversations with the people involved.

As mentioned at the beginning of this chapter, inheritance, and particularly economic inheritance, i.e. money and property, is very often a taboo subject in families. But when the future of a business depends on it, the subject becomes unavoidable and must be prepared in advance.

In the previous section, you have already analyzed the current shareholding situation. You must now know who owns the company and in what proportions. You have also made assumptions about what the company's environment might look like in 10 years thanks to the 3-circle model, of which the shareholding (ownership) was part. Unfortunately, with a topic as serious as this one, imagination will not be enough: a detailed plan will have to be drawn up and many conversations will have to be held on the subject with all family members, including those who aren't involved in the business. As we saw in Chapter 3, although the business is an entity in its own right, it's also closely tied to the family and to those who aren't shareholders. Decisions made about the ownership of the business will affect the family at large, since they'll have a direct impact on its income.

In France, for example, a business owner may decide to make a shared gift[20] to his or her children by giving shares of the business in anticipation of inheritance. Up to the age of 71, the owner can benefit from a 50% reduction in gift tax, so it's in the owner's best interest to give the business to his or her children before reaching that age. The problem is that the capital from the sale of the company often corresponds to the retirement income of the owner and that if he gives his company to his children in the form of shares, he loses the income that assured him a certain comfort for his old age...

The above example is a good illustration of the impact that each business decision can have on the family. There's no obligation for the owner to give equal shares to each of his children, so you may not have the same amount as your siblings at the moment. Everything should balance out at the time of the succession, following the death of your parents, by compensating with available personal assets or with money. Be aware, however, that the shared gift freezes the value of the business at the time it's signed. So, if you work in the business and multiply its value, your siblings will not benefit. Keep in mind

---

[20] Assistant-Juridique, *Est-il préférable de vendre ou de donner l'entreprise à ses enfants?*, 2021, [Online], URL address : https://www.assistant-juridique.fr/vente_donation_entreprise_enfants.jsp

that having shares in a business also means having rights and duties. This means that your siblings have the right to vote and have a say in the management of the family business even if they aren't involved and hold a minority stake.

In Quebec, or elsewhere, the issues remain similar even though the laws and taxation are quite different. For example, in Quebec, prior to 2016, it was more advantageous for a parent to sell his or her business to a third party rather than to his or her children. Since 2016, the tax laws have changed significantly to reverse this fact, but they don't affect all sectors of activity. Regardless, you'll need to speak with your attorneys or a tax advisor at the time you want to join the business to determine the different options available to you and choose the most advantageous one.

Share issues aren't considered a priority by families as long as everyone is getting along and the parents are healthy. But what happens when your parents die? How will the business inheritance be distributed between the children involved and those who aren't?

To avoid additional sources of conflict on all inheritance issues, discuss them with your parents today and let them make the decision. If possible, all succession transactions should be done with your parents while they're still around, so that they can decide and mediate between you and your siblings. If you don't settle the family business inheritance before your parents die, the business affairs may become mixed up with the family inheritance, which could greatly complicate the division of shares, increase the time of the transition and possibly trigger conflicts. Don't forget that the company risks being automatically divided by the number of children and that this could quickly cause panic among the employees, but also severely affect the current manager. Indeed, it's the latter that, bereaved by the death of his parents, will have to continue to run the company while being pressured by his brothers and sisters. This is simply not an option. If you can, take the time to discuss this with your family, listen to everyone's wishes and make wise decisions. Your family is precious and the business is an asset. You owe it to yourself to prepare for the legacy from the beginning of your integration if you want what you value to last.

In the family business, the family is central. All facets of it are present in one way or another and it will be impossible to completely separate your family life from your business life. There are many good things about this, but you must not neglect the emotional burden that this situation represents. All your emotions, happy and unhappy, are multiplied tenfold. Much like being the parents of two families, you will invest a lot of personal time, energy and money, but you'll also enjoy many great moments and memories that will be passed on from generation to generation long after you're gone. You'll also develop great relationships in which your employees will become friends or even a second family.

It may seem like a huge undertaking, but all the steps will be spread out over several years and you'll gradually learn everything you need to know as you get involved. Don't be afraid to take the plunge if that's what you want!

And if you still don't feel up to it, maybe this last section will help you see things more clearly.

Step 3:

You

Chapter 7
Your personal motivations

The family

The first question to ask yourself is: who or what gave you the idea to join the family business? The second would be: why do you want to join and take over the family business?

Now that you have all the theoretical and technical tools to understand the environment and the specific issues of a family business, you're able to answer this last question with full knowledge of the facts. The only thing left to determine is the personal and professional motivations that drive your choice. And since family is at the center of your decision, you can't take it lightly and risk creating tension. Of course, you have the right to change your mind or ask for a trial period, but your intentions should be noble from the start.

The following questions will help you determine the origin of your motivation. If the idea of joining the family business comes from you, chances are your motivation is much higher than if your parents have been pushing you since your childhood to get involved when you don't want to. It's therefore important that you determine whether the idea comes from you or from your family.

Are you under pressure from your family to join the business? Is there an alternative if you decide not to take over the business? Can another family member take it over? Will the business have to be sold if no family member commits to taking over? If the interest and idea comes from you, the pressure will be much less than if your parents or other family members are urging with you to join the business.

Depending on your case, I advise you to pay particular attention to this part, because it will help you determine your deepest motivations and therefore know if this project is viable or if, on the contrary, your interest points in another direction. Be true to yourself. The stakes are high and involve your entire family and possibly the future of your employees. It's always better to be honest from the start and risk hurting a few people than to live miserably for years just to please your parents. You're an adult and therefore have the right to make your decisions regardless of their opinions. You need to let go of your emotions for a moment and affirm your choice, whatever it is. If you're sincere and your arguments are well prepared, your decision will be accepted sooner or later. If it's your parents' wish that you join the company and your final answer is no, they will most likely be disappointed or angry for a while. Even if they are, it's a risk you have to take. If you are sincere, they will come back to you at some point and may even be grateful that you didn't get involved against your will. Also, be aware that forcing someone to get involved in the business when they don't want to isn't a good strategy. Indeed, the person would probably never provide results equivalent to a truly interested person, whose motivations would be deep and genuine. So don't take this decision lightly.

Explain to your family your reasons for refusing a position with the company. Explain to them the risks they would be taking by hiring you despite your reluctance. They would lose time, money and the company's image could be tarnished in the eyes of other employees and the rest of the family. You can also suggest an alternative. If you're an only child, for example, or your siblings are already involved elsewhere, perhaps you could expand the proposal to your distant cousins. You could also take the idea back to your siblings, who might be mature enough for a career change. There are certainly solutions, and you may be surprised at the results if you take the idea and proposing it around you. Of course, these steps will also show your interest in the business and its success, even if you don't want to get personally involved.

In any case, you need to look beyond your emotions about not disappointing your parents and be mature. Think carefully about the consequences of your decision, both positive and negative. Take some time to weigh the pros and cons and ask for a trial period in an area that interests you, or spend a day with your parents to get a more concrete idea of their daily tasks.

If you're interested in taking over the family business, you can also ask yourself the same questions. How does the family impact your decision? Do you want to be involved in preserving the family legacy, for example?

You

Taking the family factor out of the equation, why do you want to join the family business? What drives you to do this?

Perhaps you have a vocation for entrepreneurship, i.e. the creation and development of businesses, but you want to put your skills to good use within the family business rather than starting from scratch. Taking over a business brings its share of challenges, just like starting a business. You'll find satisfaction in this project. Participating in the construction and development of something bigger than yourself, as a team, with people you like, gives you an incomparable sense of accomplishment and satisfaction. Maybe this is what you're looking for. But to fulfill this need for accomplishment, you'll have to work hard and your main challenge will probably be to find a balance between your professional and personal life. The notion of balancing work and family is both a challenge in terms of professional accomplishment, but also a goal you may want to set for yourself that you feel you can more easily achieve by working in the family business. This is indeed a nuance that we can explore further.

It's true that your family will be much more likely to give you time to deal with an unexpected event with your children, for example, since they'll feel directly concerned by everything that affects their grandchildren, nephews or nieces. While the situation may seem ideal in the case of unforeseen events, this doesn't necessarily mean that balancing work-family will be easy to achieve in all circumstances, quite the contrary. Since you'll spend most of your time surrounded by your family, you may not feel the need to see them outside of work. However, it's still important to voluntarily establish a work-family balance from the beginning and throughout the process. You may see your parents all day at work, but have you had a personal conversation with them recently?

Seeing your parents at work means being at work and talking about work, which isn't the same as a Saturday night family dinner. Work isn't a place to have deep private conversations and home isn't a place to have a business meeting. You must be intentional about separating the places and times you have with your family. Obviously, exceptions can occur, so be flexible when necessary. That said, to help you and your family achieve this balance, you may want to set clear rules from the beginning, such as no talking about work at home, or, if you don't live together, a requirement that you meet one Saturday a month for a family dinner.

It seems obvious that we don't have the same relationship with our work colleagues as we do with our family. However, your family will be there for all the important moments of your life and therefore deserves that you make the effort to keep a personal contact with them. In the eyes of your parents, you're still their child, so you must necessarily take into account the emotional factors when defining your work-family balance.

In the same vein, we tend to think of our time at the office as family time, but as we've just shown, it's not exactly the same thing. In addition to damaging your relationship with your family involved in the business, staying very late at the office every day, either to finish a current project or to prove your value to the company, will certainly have a negative impact on your personal life. If you have your own family, you need to make sure you give them enough attention, and if you're on your own, you need to make time for yourself to see your friends and meet someone.

The reasons that might motivate you to do the opposite are really just excuses. You DON'T have to cancel dinner with friends to finish a project and you DON'T have to prove to everyone that you're worthy of taking over the company by sending emails in the middle of the night. Your legitimacy will be earned through the quality of your work, not the hours you put in at the office. Quality work can be done during the normal hours of the workday. So don't put your life on hold.

By organizing your time in each part of your life, you will certainly find the balance that suits you. But don't forget to keep some flexibility. Yes, an emergency at work may arise from time to time and force you to stay late at the office... But not every day!

Chapter 8
Your Professional Motivations

Learning

Your personal motivation is essential to your decision to join the family business, but so are your professional motivations. Learning is probably a component of your job motivation without you necessarily being aware of it.

When you start a new job, you must necessarily develop new skills, new knowledge, to learn how to perform your tasks properly. If you want to join the family business, you'll have to learn, as in any other business, how to do your job as it's expected. And if you ever want to take over the family business, you'll need to learn your parents' business, but also learn more from your parents. It may seem daunting at first, but at the end of the day, what could be more natural than learning from our parents? They've probably already taught you how to walk, talk, helped you with your homework and guided you through your first big decisions. You've been through this process many times since you were born. And while those times may not bring back fond memories, your maturity and interest in the project will likely lead to a better experience this time around.

Don't worry about this process. You've already learned from your parents in the past and you probably did it under worse conditions, and in a worse frame of mind. In any case, your parents won't be able to spend the day with you to teach you the tricks of the trade, so you'll have to follow employees who specialize in certain tasks, who will themselves be able to pass on some important notions about working in the company. You'll have the opportunity to have different "teachers" throughout your training and throughout your career.

Be aware that your learning phase will last much longer than a few months during your induction; it'll continue throughout your career. You'll never be able to integrate knowledge from all areas of the company. You pay people every day for their work because they have the skills to do it, skills that you don't have because you haven't been through the same process as them. Your goal is indeed to have the experience to work in the company, but only for a particular position. You'll not be expected to know everyone's job perfectly. You may be expected to know the basics - the employee's role, importance, challenges, and issues, but you won't be expected to be able to fill in. If you could fill all the positions at once and very efficiently, you wouldn't have any employees!

Let's look at an example:

Your family business is a company that makes industrial cakes. You probably have pastry cooks among the work crew who make the cake mixes. During your initial training, you'll probably spend time with the bakers to talk with them, observe their work and perhaps help them. By observing them, you'll probably realize how fast they work. By talking to them, you'll discover that they sometimes work so mechanically that they struggle to explain why they do what they do, or that they are able to tell you the exact quantities of certain products. You'll learn that one of their daily challenges is to carry the several kilo bags of flour from storage to the manufacturing room. Through this experience, you'll integrate some knowledge (information, data), but you'll certainly won't be able to develop any skills or knowledge of how to be a baker since you won't have done the tasks long enough. It would probably take a few more months for the word "baker" to be added to your personal skills.

As you can see, you won't be able to add all the company's jobs to your skills sheet. As a new member, you especially need to understand how the company works and what the issues are for each sector and employee. Of course, if your company is made up of a hundred areas and thousands of employees, it will be impossible for you to get to know all the people and areas before you start working. In this case, simply try to study the different sectors that exist without going into depth. Depending on the size of the company, this phase of observation or remote study may therefore take more or less time. When you start in the company, you can plan a period to simply observe and analyze each role. This will also give the different employees a chance to get to know you. In addition, they will like the fact that you're interested in them and their work.

Learning the different trades of the company, even on the surface, is essential to work there and even more so if you want to take over the company later on. Imagine that you accept an order from a customer who asks for four times as many cakes as usual within the same time limit, but you don't know the technical skills of the factory and of the employees who work there. You'll certainly encounter some problems in delivering this order on time. The delay will cost your customer money, make them unhappy and give them a bad impression of your company. Internally, tensions may arise between workers and management. Workers will have to work harder and under pressure, which can cause injuries and make workers unavailable.

Of course, all of this can be avoided by taking the time to study the workers' job and their production skills. Accept the fact that they know more about their work than you do, communicate with them and let them teach you more about their job. This will give you all the tools you need to succeed.

When you first enter the company, it's very difficult to assess your abilities and to know what you can bring to the company. This is normal. This will be part of your learning process throughout your integration process and afterwards, during the takeover phase. As you go along, you'll discover your strengths and weaknesses, what you like to do and what you don't like to do. You'll take your place and assert your usefulness, both to yourself and to your parents.

Throughout this journey, remember that you're a whole person with your own ideas, ambitions, strengths and weaknesses, even if you're the product of your parents' relationship. It's unlikely that you'll have the same ways of doing things as your parents, let alone the same skills, and that's okay. Just remember that you don't have the same experiences as your parents either. Maybe you've had an education and they haven't. Maybe they had some work experience before starting their own business or taking over their parents' business, while you decided to start your own without having worked anywhere else. All scenarios are possible. And all of these experiences have contributed, for them as well as for you, to forge specific learning that allow you to have the skills you have today. You should see the difference between your parents and yourself as a chance to complement each other and bring something new to the business. And unless you're completely off base, there's never only one way to do things to achieve the same result. So your solutions are just as legitimate as your parents'. As long as you understand how the business works, what's at stake, and you're aware of the risks you're taking, you can succeed in a different way than your parents without affecting the business.

Obviously, it isn't easy to impose new ways of doing things on your parents who have been working in the company for years and who have learned from bad experiences. They often feel that because their solution has worked for years, it's the right way to go. To make them understand that other equally good solutions are possible, you'll need to be patient and strategic in bringing your ideas as suggestions that you would like to test as part of your learning. Present your project and discuss it with them while remaining open. If they show you logically that your project can't work, don't just implement something that is likely to fail. On the other hand, if they're simply reluctant to take a measured risk, try to find ways to minimize the risk. Present your project to them as an opportunity for you to prove yourself and the company what you're capable of. That said, there's no need to get angry and cause conflict. Creating a new project, no matter how big or small, should be an exciting adventure dedicated to improving one aspect of the business. If you improve one aspect, but damage your relationship with your parents in the process, the value of your idea will be less.

In any case, just remember that you're different from your parents and therefore your management approach will be different from theirs, which isn't a problem. You will develop many skills that will fit your personality. And that is how you will make your family business history.

Perspectives

In a family business, you can expect higher work motivation than elsewhere. Work motivation depends mainly on five factors: compensation, job content, working conditions, work relationships and status. Since people are at the heart of the family business, your compensation, benefits and working conditions are also likely to be higher than those of the competition. If you wish, your position can be tailor-made and you'll be able to fully develop yourself on a daily basis with tasks that are similar to yours. Since you'll be working with your family, your relationships at work will be fulfilling and happy, most of the time. Finally, as a member of the family, you'll have a privileged status in the company, from the moment you arrive.

The picture painted here is very general and may, of course, vary by company and your expectations in each area. Not all of these areas will be equally satisfied at all times. There will be times when your relationships at work won't be satisfactory, or you'll be working on a project that you're less happy with. But in the grand scheme of things, and by evaluating these criteria over the course of your career in the family business, the various aspects can certainly all be met in a meaningful way. If you're motivated to give the best of your abilities and skills, your integration as well as your career could be more successful than you expect.

If you join the family business as a family member, your career prospects for the position and salary may be high. If you have the desire and work hard, you could eventually step into your parents' shoes and take over the business. Of course, this isn't everyone's goal. You may well want to enter the family business without necessarily wanting to take it over. It's possible to thrive in a specific area of the business and want to stay there without hoping to climb the corporate ladder. The general idea is that you find your place and that you're good at what you do. So no matter what position you're aiming for, you need to ask yourself if this position can best help you to contribute to the company's long-term success.

Not everyone wants to run a company. On the other hand, everyone can run a company if they develop certain knowledge: know-how and interpersonal skills. This is part of the learning process we discussed earlier in this chapter. To develop knowledge, for example, you can acquire a minimum of abilities about each area of the company's activities, even if they don't interest you. For example, you can learn to read financial statements in order to propose strategies to improve the company's financial health. To develop multiple skills, you can start by developing your political skills, as discussed in Chapter 3, so that you don't mix private and professional conflicts in the company.

As you can see, all of these skills can be developed and any human being is capable of learning them. Of course, it'll take time, experience and you'll certainly make mistakes before you master them even partially. But if you're motivated to take over the business, you'll manage to develop all the necessary skills during your training. It'll be hard, it'll take a lot of work, but if you put in the necessary effort and you're willing to learn, you'll eventually be able to take on the job you want.

You have been lucky enough to be in the leadership race since birth. Like in royalty, your place is kept for you. But, unlike the kings, you have the choice to accept it or not and no one can blame you for not wanting it. It's an opportunity; not an obligation. And if it's not your career goal to get there, if you have other plans elsewhere or internally, you have the right to pursue your goals. If you're not happy in your work, whatever it may be, you won't perform well and will eventually harm your team, yourself and, in the case of a family business, your family.

You should also be aware that there are probably managers in every area of the company, and if you're interested in a particular area, you may want to consider becoming an area manager. If there's no area that interests you, but you have an evolving project, you could become a project manager instead. Depending on the size of the company, there are several avenues that are independent of management, and you may find your niche in between. Keep an open mind, observe and ask people to show you what they do all day. They will likely appreciate your interest in them and their work and will be happy to provide you with information. If the project or sector you would like to work in doesn't exist, create it! This is called intrapreneurship*. If your project is in line with the family business and can add value to it, why not give it a try? It's through this type of initiative that companies grow and increase in value. Put your project together and present it to your parents. If they see your enthusiasm and feel that the risks are minimal, they may agree to let you go ahead with your project!

> ***Definition - Intrapreneurship:** the action of undertaking or setting up a project within a company.

The ultimate goal is for you to find a position in the company that matches your personality and career ambitions. You may go through different functions that you don't like as much before you really find your place. Don't give up, there are plenty of opportunities available to you. Your goals may also change over time, taking you in unexpected directions! Keep an open mind throughout your integration and succession process. It's never too late to discover your passions, no matter what your age.

In conclusion, not everyone is cut out to take over a business, but everyone can have a place in the family business.

Conclusion

The purpose of this book is to provide you with some pointers to help you decide if joining a family business would be a good solution for you. Like any project, there are advantages and disadvantages to work in a family business, and we have more or less covered them. Your choice will be based on your ability to ignore one or the other. Based on the information you've been given throughout these pages, do you see more advantages or more disadvantages?

In the end, only you will be able to tell if this project is right for you or not. Remember that no matter what your parents' wishes are, the decision you make at the end of the adventure is yours and should make you happy. The worst thing you could do, for yourself and for your parents, would be to make a decision that doesn't come from your heart. By reluctantly embarking on a project you're not excited about, you may be able to hide your unhappiness for a while, but tensions between you and your parents will inevitably resurface. Obviously this situation won't benefit anyone.

On the other hand, it's also possible that even with the best will in the world, your integration won't work. It's not easy to work with family. Your parents may say they're ready but may not feel ready to integrate you. Parents often associate their children coming into the family business with their own withdrawal from it. They begin to think about what's ahead "after the business" without necessarily wanting to, and also see retirement approaching at a speed they don't always like. They will go through a range of emotions during your onboarding, which may, depending on their personality, alter your relationship. These may be normal, superficial tensions that will diminish over time, but deeper arguments may also erupt, causing a breach of the moral contract you had with them. And that breach would, of course, mean the end of your integration and the end of the takeover project.

Unfortunately, these things happen even with the best of intentions; hence the importance of managing emotions that arise along the way before they explode and damage the project. The best way to do this is through communication. Talk to your parents and don't be afraid to be vulnerable on both sides. You can also hire an outside person, a mediator, like the family council, to ease tensions, promote healthy communication and guide you through the process.

An external event, such as an economic crisis, can also destabilize your integration process by causing an economic loss for your company or even its closure. Obviously, these catastrophic scenarios are isolated cases, but it's important to mention the internal and external risks that could thwart your plans. There's other risks that can affect your journey, such as a family member who doesn't want you to join the company, or your dismissal from the company.

Think about the other risks you may face in your business. This will help you find ways to reduce these risks before you make or announce your decision.

Remember that there's always a solution to your problem. Be creative and enjoy every moment; there's a great family adventure ahead of you.

Acknowledgments

To Mathilde Rossi, my best friend and my greatest support for the past 15 years in all my ideas and projects. I wish you the best of success in New York!

To my friends and my pre-launch team, Liora Lehmann, Elise Priolet, Lara Pegliasco and Julie Perronnet who did everything to help me make this project a reality, combining their talents and strengths. I am very grateful to have these strong and independent women as my friends.

A special thanks to Liora Lehmann for designing the book cover. Thank you for listening and being patient.

A big thank you to my editor Elyzabeth Martel-Choinière and translator Cathia Nemours for the incredible work they did on the book.

A huge thank you to the entire team of Familles en Affaire HEC Montréal and its sponsors for the creation of the program: Circuit - Sur la voie de la Relève. A special thanks to Mélissa Laflamme-Ouellet and Annie Veilleux for facilitating the meetings and for their precious support. Without this program, I would never have had the idea for this book and my career would surely have taken a different path.

A special thank you to Luis-Felipe Cisneros, Scientific Director of the Entrepreneurship, Repreneurship and Family Business Pole, and Professor of Entrepreneurship at HEC Montréal, for pushing me to enroll and for taking his time to revise my manuscript.

A big thank you to my mentoring group from the M Network, to my mentor Louise Lefebvre for her wise advice and to my classmates Katia, Stéphanie and François, for their exchange and frankness.

Thank you to my family for inspiring me.

Thank you to all the people who shared this book to support me.

Thank you, reader, for choosing this book and for keeping an open mind about the family business.

Your reference guide

Now that you've finished reading this book, you should be familiar with the three major steps in the decision-making process that will lead you to determine whether or not the family business is right for you: the business itself, the family and you. However, the various topics and themes that have been covered in this book may have left you feeling a little nervous about what you need to do next to make your decision. This is normal! To help you in your decision-making process, arm yourself with this practical checklist and follow the steps in order. I even invite you to detach it from the book so that you can use it as a reference throughout your adventure.

Good luck and, above all, have fun!

1. Do your research on the company

The first step in your questioning process is to learn a little bit about the company. What industry is it in? What do they sell? What type of business is it? How does it operate?

In this first step, there is no need to go too far with a complete analysis. You'll discover all the details of the operation little by little. Do your research as if you were interviewing for a job, knowing that you'll be able to ask all the questions you want during your integration. To find the information you need to get started, you can check out your company's website, which is a great place to start your research. If your company doesn't have a website or it doesn't have a lot of information, your only option is to ask your parents directly. You'll need to have a conversation with them at some point, in step 3. However, if you manage to gather enough information on your own, you can move on to Step 2 by completing the exercises. You'll cover all the details of the business in depth in Step 3.

2. Draw your 3-cricle model

We explored the 3-circle model in the early chapters of this book and you may have already done the exercise while reading. If so, you can always go back to it or review it. After reading this book in it's entirely, you'll have gained a more complete understanding of a family's business environment and you may find that your model needs modification. If you haven't yet built your 3-circle model, now is the time to do so. Remember that the model is made up of 3 overlapping circles, representing the different environments of a family in business. The first circle represents the family, the second circle represents the business, and the third circle represents the ownership. The purpose of the exercise is to note the names of the people involved in the corresponding circles. If people are involved in more than one circle, you must place them where the circles overlap. In the end, your model should give you an idea of the different actors connected to the family business and the links between them. This exercise will go a long way in helping you to understand the business environment and to see where the challenges and opportunities lie for your integration.

3. Have a conversation with your parents

This is probably the most important and terrifying step: you need to talk to your parents about your plans to join the family business. Whether it's coming to watch and learn more or taking over the business, talking about your interest in a planned conversation is key. If you don't talk to your parents, you simply won't be able to move forward with your plan. This conversation is important because it's the first one you'll undertake with your knowledge and desire in mind, but also because you'll have to ask all the questions you don't have answers for. You'll be in a vulnerable position, which is never very pleasant, but remember that your fate depends on the outcome of this conversation with your parents. Without their agreement, your project will fall through. Rest assured, unless there's exceptional circumstances, your parents are unlikely to say no. But be patient. They may not jump with excitement right away. This conversation, if it's the first one you've had, may come as a surprise to them, and they'll probably need some time to digest the information and understand what it means to them.

4. Spend a day at the company

If the conversation went well, perhaps you were able to ask to spend a day with your parents in the field, if they didn't offer it on their own. In any case, spending a day, a week or a few days a month at the company is necessary to understand its day-to-day activities. If you're still wondering if you would like to work in the family business, this step is crucial. By visualizing the daily activities of your parents and employees, you'll be better at figuring out if you could fit into the business. If you already know that you want to, taking a few days to observe before jumping in can help you gain some perspective. This may be your last chance to see the company from the outside, so take notes on what you see, what you'd like to improve, change or add. These notes can always be useful in creating plans during your onboarding process. This is what will help you fit in and bring your own culture to the company, and later, make the succession process easier.

5.   Ask yourself the right questions

After all these steps, you should have enough knowledge to know whether you want to join the family business or not. Of course, you'll still have some questions, fears or doubts before you take the plunge, but perhaps you'll decide to try out a short period of time. There's nothing to stop you from starting with an internship or a summer job, but be aware that you should still try out a probation period in the company, especially if you still have doubts. When you decide to join the company and make this commitment towards your parents, you'll sign a moral contract together that will commit you and your parents to invest in the adventure so that it'll be a successful one. The stakes are high, you will have to make every effort with your parents to make this integration work and they will have to do the same. And since the stakes will be high, the disappointments will be just as much. Take it easy on yourself and your family. You don't have to join the family business, no matter what anyone tells you.

There are always alternatives, and the decision is ultimately yours. If, after your probationary period, you realize that you're not interested in joining the family business or you're no longer interested, tell your parents and move on, but don't pretend.

Appendix: The different legal business status in France[21]

	Partner(s)	Manager(s)
Sole proprietorship (EI) Sole proprietorship with limited liability (EIRL)	The individual entrepreneur	The individual entrepreneur
One-man business with limited liability (EURL)	One individual and one legal entity	One or more managers (individuals)
Société à responsabilité limitée (SARL)	2 to 100 individuals or legal entities	One or more managers (individuals)
Société anonyme (SA)	At least 2 physical or moral entities (or 7 for companies listed on the stock exchange)	A board of directors of 3 to 18 members, with a president appointed among them
Société par actions simplifiées (SAS) Société par actions simplifiée unipersonnelle (SASU)	Minimum of one individual or legal entity	A president (individual or legal entity), obligation of a legal representative

---

[21] Bercy Info, *Quel Statut juridique choisir pour son entreprise?*, Ministère de l'économie des finances et de la relance, 2019, [En ligne], adresse URL : https://www.economie.gouv.fr/entreprises/entreprise-choisir-statut-juridique#

Société en nom collectif (SNC)	At least 2 individuals or legal entities	One or more managers (individuals or legal entities)
La société coopérative de production (SCOP)	Employees of the enterprise (up to a minimum of 51% of the capital) and possibly external investors	A director or manager elected by the majority partners
Société en commandite par actions (SCA)	At least 4 partners, including 1 general partner and 3 limited partners	One or more managers (individual or legal entities) appointed by the general partners s)
Société en commandite simple (SCS)	At least 2 partners, including 1 general partner and 1 limited partner	One or more managers (individual or legal entities) appointed by the general partners)

Bibliography

Reference books

BEAUCAGE, C., PARÉ-JULIEN, D., *Le petit guide de la famille en affaires – Le conseil de famille*, Éditions JFD, Montréal, 2020, 40 p.

Circuit – Sur la voie de la relève, « La gouvernance », [notes taken as part of the Le Circuit program], HEC Montréal, Montréal, February 2020

CISNEROS, L., *La Gouvernance*, Circuit – Sur la voie de la relève, PowerPoint presentation, HEC Montréal, 2020

CISNEROS, L., HAMON, G., VEILLEUX, A., GUILIANI, F., IBANESCU, M., *L'album de familles — enquête statistique sur les entreprises familiales québécoises 2020*, Familles en affaires — HEC Montréal, 2021

COLLINS, Jim, *Built to Last : Successful Habits of Visionary Companies*, 3e éd., New York, Harper Business, 1994, 368 p.

DAVIS, J., TAGIURI, R., *The Influence of Life Stages on Father-Son Work Relationships in Family Companies*, Unpublished manuscript, Graduate School of Business Administration, University of Southern California, 1982, 924 p.

KENYON-ROUVINEZ, D., WARD, J. L., *L'importance de la gouvernance familiale et de la gouvernance entrepreneuriale*, dans *Les entreprises familiales*, Presses Universitaires de France, 2004, 127 p.

LAINEY, P., *Les habiletés politique*, Circuit – Sur la voie de la relève, PowerPoint presentation, HEC Montréal, 2020

WHITESIDE, M., ARONOFF, C., WARD, J., *How families work together*, 2e éd., Family Business Consulting Group Publications, New York, 1993, 99 p.

Websites

Assistant-Juridique, *Est-il préférable de vendre ou de donner l'entreprise à ses enfants?*, 2021, [Online], URL address : https://www.assistant-juridique.fr/vente_donation_entreprise_enfants.jsp

BASSETT ET FORBES, *The Economic Impact of Family-Owned Enterprise in Canada*, 2019, [Online], URL address: https://familyenterprise.ca/wp-content/uploads/2020/01/CBOC-2019-Family-Owned-Enterprises-Impact-Report.pdf

Bercy Info, *Quel Statut juridique choisir pour son entreprise?*, Ministère de l'économie des finances et de la relance, 2019, [Online], URL address: https://www.economie.gouv.fr/entreprises/entreprise-choisir-statut-juridique#

COLLINS, J., *Vision Framework*, JimCollins.com, 2001, [Online], URL address: https://www.jimcollins.com/tools/vision-framework.pdf

Familles en Affaires, *Circuit – Sur la voie de relève*, Famille en Affaires, HEC Montréal, 2021, [Online], URL address: https://famillesenaffaires.hec.ca/circuit/#_circuit-programmation-anchor

Familles en Affaires, HEC Montréal, 2021, [Online], URL address: https://famillesenaffaires.hec.ca/

KINDERMANS, M., *BPI France se mobilise pour la survie des entreprises familiales*, Les Échos, 2020, [Online], URL address: https://www.lesechos.fr/pme-regions/actualite-pme/bpifrance-se-mobilise-pour-la-survie-des-entreprises-familiales-1162454

Québec, *Démarrer votre entreprise*, Registraire des entreprises Québec, 2017, [Online], URL address : http://www.registreentreprises.gouv.qc.ca/fr/demarrer/constituer-pmsbl.aspx

RASMUS, D. W., *Defining your company's Vision*, Fast Company, 2012, [Online], URL address: https://www.fastcompany.com/1821021/defining-your-companys-vision

Contents

Thank you

for purchasing my book

Please feel free to leave a review on Amazon and join the worker with family community on Facebook:

www.facebook.com/groups/workingwithyourfamily.travaillerenfamille/